Pelagic Mania

poems by

Willard P. Greenwood II

Finishing Line Press
Georgetown, Kentucky

Pelagic Mania

Copyright © 2017 by Willard P. Greenwood II
ISBN 978-1-63534-213-0 First Edition
All rights reserved under International and Pan-American Copyright Conventions.
No part of this book may be reproduced in any manner whatsoever without written permission from the publisher, except in the case of brief quotations embodied in critical articles and reviews.

ACKNOWLEDGMENTS

Riseforms (online journal), "Cabin Fever Sickness" February 2012
The Art of Angling: Poems About Fishing, "Gravedigger," 2011.
"Vermont Hardware Store Fly-Rod" and "The Evening Troll" appeared in *The Yale Angler's Journal*, 2007
"The Western Shore" appeared in *The Listening Eye* 2003
"Pelagic Mania" appeared in *The Seneca Review*, April 2002
"Quaking Bog" appeared in *Passages North*, Winter/Spring 2001
"Dead Water" appeared in *Poem* No. 79, 1998

Publisher: Leah Maines

Editor: Christen Kincaid

Cover Art: Rebecca Smetak

Author Photo: Yvonne Sherwood

Cover Design: Elizabeth Maines McCleavy

Printed in the USA on acid-free paper.
Order online: www.finishinglinepress.com
    also available on amazon.com

        Author inquiries and mail orders:
           Finishing Line Press
            P. O. Box 1626
        Georgetown, Kentucky 40324
              U. S. A.

Table of Contents

Vermont Hardware Store Fly-Rod 1

Maine Spring of 1993 2

Dead Water 3

Pelagic Mania 5

The Western Shore of Ferry Beach 7

Quaking Bog 8

Gravedigger 10

Winslow Homer 12

Victory Beer Poem in a Grand Laker Canoe 14

Ode to an Unnamed Pond 16

Cabin Fever Sickness 18

A Fishing Trip in Early May 20

Portage Wheels 21

The Evening Troll 23

Lost Pond 26

The Last Lust Striper 28

Blue Flags, Wild Irises 29

For Beth

Vermont Hardware Store Fly-Rod

In the unvarnished good old days of carp,
We left the morning's giant iron stove
Heating the farmhouse brooding by the tarp
That kept the ice off the VW's trove
Of fishing gear, gear for rainbow trout.

My regular dad bought this stuff for us.
I was five and clothed enough to go out
Into the unheated weather of the bus.
I had fished green hand-lines behind the house,
So my training with that odd limber thing
Made me mad and weak as a mouthy mouse.
He yelled at me. You should have seen him bring
The redhorse, gasping to the streambed's shore,
In the twilight year, 1974.

Maine Spring of 1993

Pathetic and desperate for any moving creature,
the urge to fish in cold weather
nosed itself toward me in the bleak climate of Gorham, Maine.
I used the pain
of those two medicated guys
who said they were Vietnam Veterans
to fish the small trestle on Lake Sebago.
Their own teeth were worn down and broken off.
The creosote of the trestle's heavy brown timbers
seeped into their gums.
Biting back at black mornings by fishing,
before the sun hit
I heard them talking—
when, Shit, O, Shit, the waters around the trestle were cold,
reallyreally deeply freezing cold
and I, my unemployed self, just sort of slipped into them for the dropped fly-rod
—supercheap gear—something my father bought in the 1970s,
somehow worth going into 34 degree water on a 22 degree morning.

Their sort of friendly cackling hack laughing
almost shattered my teeth.
I was freezing
before I waded to my chest for the cruddy rod
barely floated by the line in the crappy five dollar Martin Reel
and grabbed at the sunken green fly-line
billowing underwater
in huge intestinal loops.

Dead Water

Somewhere I have come from to here
over crotch hooking barbed wire
past mildewed poles sad with rot
to wonder an undercut riverbank.

White pine overhangs shade depths
meandering to the dappled shallows
of dace and chub darting from kingfishers.
A snapping turtle extends its neck
longer than its prehistoric body.

I cast the hornberg to mossy brows,
reel up and head for the deeper pools
where the river slows and bends
through shifting sand and mud.

My way unwinds among vast trunks of pine.

The river's slow crook holds trunks and limbs,
gone white in the sun. Yellow pollen clots
in the ache of slow eddies.

Furtive rustle, perhaps behind or up ahead.

The green line goes out easily
lets the leader curl perfectly.
The retrieve—joyful stop
is just some corpse of a stuck log.

A squirrel leaps and hangs
swaying on a branch.

Heaving and hoping to re-tie
and salvage a brown trout from the twilight,
my straight pull moves something,
and bone snap, the whole mess comes
popping back tangled in the sandy grit at my feet.
The hornberg glints, sinking,
hooked to something awful,
in the slow gathering river.

Pelagic Mania

There (where I was)
the forthrightness
of beach pebbles was being cobbled
by the tidal back and forthness
of the sun, then moon
and throughout the nighttime Gigantomachea
won by mosquitoes.
Waving nine feet of graphite
tethered with monofilament to strange love,
was me—
with a protective slime of fish solitude,
sun-block, bug dope, old sweat,
and wet shoes—
making penultimate casts
into each fishless hour of gloom.

The godwonderful speckled blackness,
and the line catching seaweed
meant I was fishing for stripers
that have swum by me for years.

This year's months, days, and hours
go bye without a big dead bloody thing
to mark them.

I shall chuck the whole
non-catching fish rig into the void,
but the tide would tangle the whole mess
for someone else to fix.

Mouth froth, thinking wrinkles,
and a somnolent wakefulness to match
the timesuck
of this art.

The rest of the clock belongs to despair,
and the rest of the air readies itself
For me to say
OOOOO,
what kind of dawn is that?

The Western Shore of Ferry Beach

is the low-tide wet desert
of Scarborough River's ebb.

Shallow waters cover gray heavy sand
alive with clam worms and sand eels.
The glass tablet
of high tide's evening water
is unwritten by the wind.

Out of the dark, a mile or so up the coast,
past the rivermouth, out in the night,
overdeveloped Old Orchard Beach glares with teeming fun.
The monochrome shimmering of the baubled coast
flashes like God trolling a Silver Doctor.
The gaudy, crass shining of that amusement park
pleases me more than if I were the first human
to have looked upon this river.

Fishing a sand eel fly on heavy gear:
the shank between the two hooks is 150 pound monofilament.
The water smells like dusk, like big stripers are waiting for something
to stir.
Balancing, casting from a spindly canoe, anchored with a milk jug of
sand.
Only the breath of a tapering wind and me pulling line through the
water moves the canoe.
       I have forgotten what I was writing about.
Was it waiting or fishing?
The breeze halts—
mosquitoes and black flies track me by my breath.
Black flies drop acid to burn holes in my skin,
and poke their heads in to suck bleeding pocks
that are flowing like this sea-river of salt-water,
which is feeding the salt marsh's larval universe.

Quaking Bog

Drawn and tripping so happy
down the barely worn muskrat path
leading to three acres of water
that I put the fly-reel on backward.

One gift hour from my hiking family,
and I casted my line like a god in a mortal world
to the wild trout of this mountain island
and let the line go soft along the bog edge.
We—the pond, me, and the bog—all shook.
A feeder creek wandered through
delicate growth creeping over the water,
looking for the pond's heart, the glacial spring.
I halted the god of bogs, tearing at his sedge,
standing and shifting toward rising trout.

The painted turtles collected themselves
at this blasphemy, and the minnows stopped darting.
Their bodies spelled and calculated
things about the micro-cosmos of What.

Big snapper, old gray mossback sent by the spring
to eavesdrop like the hikers across the pond
who said, "look, he's got one."
They didn't see the other two brookies I caught.

The trout were eating bugs too small to see,
so I tied a #8 hornberg
on the wrong handed reel
and after one minnow bog hour
I said WILLARD,
you have to go, to find your child
and wife. Your speckled love
will stay here. You have to exit trout
and exit island mountain pond
and since then I AM,
with weird quaking,
trying to get you back.

Gravedigger

Across big riverwater, the moon
sank below Bradley cemetery's statuary.
      A flashlight attached somebody
to the rest of the black earth.
      I used to want a job.

The hordes of Atlantic salmon
will never return. Their double digit runs
are the endangered province of the State.
      We have made it thus.

      Where did you go?
I'm talking to myself
but I mean you, and her,
and the runs of 1792.

In the half-living river,
the Undertaker
 held in the current,
sweeping out to the long
miles and messes of islands
at the Penobscot's terminus,
searching for the illicit bite.

My son went to sleep for the babysitter.
I wanted a woman to call
as I was putting on chest waders.

Caddis flies cover my fate.
Bats want to eat me.
The dark tremolo of water over rocks
are all that remains of what has not been my time on earth.

The light
across the river
won't go out. Who needs
to be buried tonight? Who had to be dug up
tonight? What dread inquest has
brought our lives together?

I pulled my feet
out of the gravel,
out of the riverbed crud
to rest on this trespass.

Winslow Homer

You painted the ocean
Surrounding the mushroom called Prouts Neck,
The weird peninsula once crowded with hotels—this is their epitaph.
There is only the Black Point Inn and here I am
Serving drinks to people eating trout
And living, because someone survived The French and Indian War.

Before the Revolutionary War
English built on two islands in the ocean,
Stratton and Bluff, before you painted jumping trout.
Indians paddled out from Prouts Neck
To kill those from whom I am
Somewhat removed. Their epitaph

Is an island chimney. An inscribed millstone epitaph
Marks Scottows Fort—all defenders killed in the war.
In these guilty woods, do you know who I am?
Who covets your crushing ocean?
Who has fled Prouts Neck
For reprints of water colored brook trout?

Seeing the *Gulf Stream* I am,
Beyond the simple fate of trout
Framed by the ocean,
That sublime aquarium of an epitaph.
You died, and the Great War
Spared your studio on Prouts Neck.

A submarine tower was built on Prouts Neck
To scan for the Wolfpack, and I am
Told that no one saw anything in The Second World War.
Where was *Casting for a Rise*? Did you tie trout?
Flies? I don't want to know your epitaph.
It probably says nothing about the ocean.

The ocean hides sea-run trout and
I am your unread epitaph,
A cold war with Prouts Neck.

Victory Beer Poem in a Grand Laker Canoe

The empty, fasted stomach clears my head of last night,
When the fire and keg of homebrew drew magnificent shadows
on another discussion of large lost fish and hooks in eyebrows—

"I could have gotten that out."

Before now we performed other
delicate operations
the leaving, the tying of flies during the long winter,
the planning, the ferrying of gear,
and the pitching of tents
to get ready for the first day's golden hour.

During this morning's paddle for boulder field brookies,
A few beers are lolling and rolling
in the stern's aquarium of overnight rainwater.

The splash behind the canoe, and, "brookies never jump like that…

It is important to enjoy life.

Beer on an empty stomach readies us to use our butter knives
properly
For the delicacy of a brook trout fried in bacon fat.
  Cheers to the passing years.
Such is the reward for landing a large brook trout
Before 6am.

In our genteel subcult of trolling flat-liners,
There is no skill, only will
And the thrill to kill the swill that is Old
Milwaukee,

The beverage that vanquishes the usual breakfast—
we belly up to the bar of the world.

The beer thickens the pond's fog

And the very clear idea of a big trout, caught quietly
By just paddling.

The big trout
dead between my feet in the bottom of the Grand Laker,
heads us toward yesterday's cold iron skillet,
greased with and for animal saints.

Ode to an Unnamed Pond

Your wading moose, your fly-bitten swimming moose,
your loon gone loony at the noonday sun's eagle,
your waterspout that nearly lifted the empty cooler
from amidships of the Old Town canoe,
your distance from all friendly towns,
your campless shores
gave us something

during our commutes
when the radio was out of music.

Your brook trout
supplanted the venison sausage
in the heroic cooler—
O Brave Cooler, how we filled
thee with the pond's late spring ice and brotherly beer.

During the casting, during the sitting and casting in high winds
and then not high winds, and when the winds were just right
at the narrow neck of the pond, where the clear water in this
moose trodden, eagle scoured, loon vacated pond,
springs forth—it was there and during those hours of casting and talk
that we caught your brook trout.

They were in the cooler on the friendly ice.
We carefully kept our limit. We drank our limit,
which is not the same thing. The sun pummeled our heads,

which we used to look at all the rocks stuck forever in shallow water.

You should see the list of stuff I made for the trip out here this year.
If I photocopied it for you, it would look like the clouds of muck that
the paddles occasionally stir from this future bog.

We caught a lot
of brook trout, and this is a grand subject in
These years of full time jobs,
marriages to genius-supermodels, sick children,
little league games, deer hunting on the Vineyard,
and long drives from Ohio to Maine
to these Gothic Maine ponds with their decomposing log rafts,
chert fashioned by human hands, bateaux skeletons,
ballast stones, collapsed canvas Old Towns,
and stashed jon-boats,
with particle board hulls that bubble underfoot.

We took no pictures.

This year
we hauled our own canoe in, so we could stay afloat.
The canoe's re-caned seats allowed us
to behold a huge brookie steam up from the depths
to eat a half-digested sucker
that a small brookie coughed up as we were landing it.

We had an onion bag of rocks for an anchor.

How big was that fish with the dead milk-bone sucker in its maw?
Bigger than any we caught.

Fly fishing can be beautifully complicated
but that day with the wind
It was just
Mickey
Finn, the kind you tied in junior high. The rusty one that you still
have in that old fly box.

The vacation is over. The Beer, professionally chilled, is all gone.
We left the rocks for you.
We must Go Home.
We are missed.

Cabin Fever Sickness

I went to the woods
with Moo Shu Beef leftovers
in January,
craving a deep pool to fish
before the State restocked the river.

No litter or foot worn path,
nothing but the crunch of snow's crust
and the lung-burn of cold air guided me.
The riparian canopy,
dimmed the glare of snowfields.
The bleak light seemed tired of me.
The violent green of un-snowed on moss,
and black bark on leeward trunks,
stark against the land's white over-belly.

Break in river ice,
good current over gravel beds
for spawning trout.
Would the Spring water be deep enough,
would the gravel bar be big enough to hide fry with their yolk sacs?

In this rheumatoid afternoon going black around Four,
non-existent trout stayed covered.
I slip-scrabbled partway
down the ledge
biting badly at a mouthful of Moo Shu,
gouging my panicked tongue.

Still,
this overhang might shadow a spot
deep enough for stocked trout to survive the winter.
A good air-flow tumbled into the pool.

I left the brook trout alone down there,
over the crayfish buried under rock and mud,
where there may be nothing but my mind and stone in the dark

In warm weather,
I'd be on the gentle side
casting to the pool
watching light slip from the world
below the river's surface,
and seeing the bank above,
where a red salamander
tumbles in, disappears with a flash,
and if that could happen,
I would continue walking the earth.

A Fishing Trip in Early May

Ended with my exultant
rock and roll arm out the truck window.
Having made future plans with my high school friends,
my mind, wired to the satellite radio waves and streamer patterns,
    used my eyes to see two girls at the side of the road who were
alone at the end of a well-kept driveway in a poor town.
    The slacker joy of a week
spent fishing and sleeping outdoors
fled at the spectre of
these
beautiful girls—
one in a backless black dress
one in a strapless white dress.
    And I felt high school again
    and am now in some 128 step program trying to recover
    from seeing them—
The fishing had been great
and the morning fog had filled me with mysteries
and a mistiness that Prom Night stripped away.
For how can they avoid the losers who will pull up to the end of the
driveway?

The girls' plotted romance and natural friendship,
without shawls, which had them bopping up and down
to keep warm on this too cool spring eve-night,
had me thinking about how great it would be if their boyfriends were
not losers, and that just a few songs earlier I had been caring
so deeply for Maxima and other
gear head things—Ah—"High School Lover" I hear you
for
last week my fancy party tux had come back from the cleaners
to date my wife's second wedding dress
in the guest room closet.

Portage Wheels

The optimal canoe load
bumps down the extinct logging road
festooned with moose browse.
The old ruts knock the wheels loose strangling
the tipping Old Town. This is not an advertisement,
but the semi-self sufficiency of the whole tableau verged on the picturesque.

The load of
firewood, five gallons of water, Down East rod holders,
Slovenian sausages, food, stove, coffee pot, tent, sleeping bag,
got re-set for the rest of the haul
and for the paddle to the eastern shore.

No Gas, no motor, I am a low-tech wunderkind.
I fish early.
in thirty eight degrees, in
a good breeze, sleet, rain, snow.

If the smelt are pimpling and
a togue hits the floating Dr. Oatman in 57 feet
of water, I might lose the whole load, the food,
the fishing journal to write it in by the one-man fire,
where the wolf-less shadows creep.
Who was Dr. Oatman?

I'm already missing Marie, but that's how my line runs these days
and in these quiet hours
I speak with her mind and body. She understands.

On the way across the Thomas & Thomas jumped in the rod holder.
A lively boil fifty feet behind the canoe—
I fight the togue. I lose the togue,
but cheat death by not drowning.
Tomorrow, I'll fish near outlets in shallow water.

The small fire with the journal
fills the abandoned woods.
The wild trout here
understand long nights.

My evening sits
atop an esker
with some moose scapulars.
Swollen freshets
accompany the night's
quiet vermiculations.

I have made it. Maker's Mark in the dark, cut with corn snow.
I am alone. Twig-fired coffee in the morning.

The early morning hours are brook trout hours.
I am in the canoe when the moon sets and the dark's blue
is unreal, surreal, real. I paddle to the ancient boulder field
 to cast for

some hook-jawed, moss-backed monster,
a living ghost of Maine's giant brook trout,
a destroyer of legends.

The Evening Troll

We lugged the boats through the woods
With cases of beer,
That our attorney had advised us to purchase,
And left loads of gear
On the shore in the Blue-Ribbon hurry to reach the water.
As the sunset gained the tasty detail of slab bacon,
The canoe carried us
Toward the boulder field's drop-off,
Toward its darkness that it had been keeping from us all year long,
Toward the western side of the lake (which is a pond)
Toward the abandoned logging camp,
But that was not this evening's destination.

   Years have collapsed the foundation walls—
The deep depression
Could receive a retiree.
The Grand Laker Canoe draws less than in its unknown heyday,
Its rotten gunnels having been
Sawed away. Having survived the decade of destruction,
We savor the direct deposits of the 30's,
Yet the grandfathered cabin on the far shore
Will not be for us when we are older.

   The monstrous esker has not disappeared into the dusk.
Trolling a large Mickey Finn
For brook trout in the boulder field can cure any hangover.
There will be an afterlife to gather all this: the very fact that we can fish,
The trout, the beer, the comfortable silence, the canoe, the trance of the troll,
The evening that still sees the camp unset on the far beach, where one of the boats has
Returned and someone is burning a tiny spot out of the night.

The man at the motor's tiller
Salvaged the 1938 Grand Laker
From some defunct Piscataquis abode.
We are dredging the pond with sinking fly line. We could
Do this forever, but let's not be romantic about life, we have 30 able springs left.
Next Year we will have 29 and so on. Perhaps we will lose the taste for road sodas.
Maybe we won't come here anymore.
The pond will keep the beer cold.

The months of winter tinkering had pulled this country into my mind.
The togue, at the end of the sinking line,
Hammered me back into myself.
The poem can hold a big fish.
And, Dear Me, it did not like the net, which caught
Only the tandem streamer, and thus the great thing hung off the outside edge
And was sort of golfed into future stories.
The album has pictures of last year's fish,
Yet the cosmic incompetence of that one remains.
Be patient.
Loose fish,
Stay in the office of my early morning phone calls.

     This evening
The troll and the idea of the troll
Disclose the clear fathoms
Where the giant esker
Meets the water.
I will never buy anything again.
I will fix the magnificent reels and tinker
With the crappy ones until I am free of money.

    We trolled up to the esker—it pointed us from the deep waters,
Into the night, where the yelling and whooping
Around the high fire,
Guided the long troll back to the beach.
And then, with our slow turn,
A mountain emerged from the pond,
Haunted by the unborn.

Lost Pond

Like Ishmael slowly falling astern the sinking Pequod
Was the PBR sixer trailing astern our square stern canoe—
A practice that we were practicing for the warmer days ahead.

The air of this lost pond was chilly enough
To chill the canned beer secured by our silly amateur lanyard.
Pale Geraldo and I were waiting
For shore lunch—we were waiting for a hunch
To tell us that our windburns
Had earned us distinction among the dead
Who were trolling with us.

We were trolling some classic streamers,
Gray Ghosts, Black Ghosts and Nine-Threes
With Floating Line in early April .

And so it was that we were trolling for
The big ones with patterns from the long dead tiers.

O, Pale Geraldo!
Your just dead Math Professor Dad
Was with us in our sober speech.
Your just buried Dad
Would be observed once
We had beached for shore lunch.

The lore of the old tiers and your Dad's pure mind
Would preside over the saint of the small fire
That warmed store bread,
Chicken, and our bare hands.

At least, we had not quit drinking.
In vino veritas, and re-hab is for quitters,
Which is why we trolled into the cold dark
And thus were not quite sure where we had parked
The truck.

We had locked the keys inside, and so
There was a very good reason and plenty of time to assess
The day's mistakes and miscalculations.

The Last Lust Striper

Stripers were the myth fish of my youth
And their runs returned as I left Maine,
My magnificent Maine of my really old grandmother,
Who said to me, before she died, "I'm shrinking!"

Thus, I lost the old place with the stone foundation,
The stones quarried from the end of the beach on the
Other side of the woods from the family house. And back
Away from this stretch where the stripers came back
Was the same strand where the old hotel had sat, the old hotel,
Where I was a high school dishwasher without stripers,
Whose employee dorm was a rockin' good place for my high
School self to chug some blow-your-lunch-punch with the college
Deadhead-enders. And further down the beach, is the old studio
Where Winslow Homer painted *Leaping Trout*. Now, it's a touristy
thing. I did
Some good work along Prouts Neck—fly-fished, got kissed
By a cheerleader, ran sprints in the sand to get ready for football,
Swam in the surf after 8 hour pot washing shifts.

Now, I am gone, having never made
Enough money to save the old house, yet on my last stay there, I took my freshwater
Fly rig to the quarried cliffs, which are now just cliffs, and caught,
With my tender lust for the sheer future,
A striper, that I ate raw
With the genius goddess cheerleader
And her Vodka bikini martinis.

Blue Flags, Wild Irises

Up out of the riverbed stones
The mayfly ephemerella
Alight on stands of Blue Flags,
The Wild Irises that rise
Above and out of
The dropping river.

Now is
The time to fish for Atlantic salmon,
Albeit illegally, and thus the fishing
Was just as tasty as the larceny
Of not making breakfast for my
Lovely love.

I finished the bottle
At 437 am
And left the morning sheets in a blue wild flag
Like we had had a blue one night stand.

And I did brawl with a salmon on the fly rod,
But it was those sheer flowerlets that I brought home
To dry. I dried the petals, crushed and mixed them
With some wild river water.

I am in high school again, painting our
Wild flag of a smoking-hot one night stand.

Willard is from Maine but lives in Hiram, Ohio where he has been teaching English and Writing at Hiram College since 2001. He lives with his wife Beth and two sons Robert and Michael. His oldest son Max lives in Maine. He teaches a legendary course called The Ethos and Practice of Fly Fishing, a writing/literature course in which students learn to fly fish. He claims that *Pelagic Mania* is the only chapbook ever published in which all the poems feature fly fishing. He has lived and fished in Indiana, Georgia, Connecticut, Vermont, Arkansas, Ohio, Maine and caught fish in Michigan, Texas, Wyoming, Montana, Idaho, Colorado and Utah.

He teaches courses on The Epics of Homer, Craft and Technique of Poetry, Sport and Literature, The Early Novels of Stephen King, American Literature and Literary Theory. He is editor-in-chief of the *Hiram Poetry Review*, which has been in continuous publication since 1966.

In addition to advanced studies on the Atlantic Ocean, Penobscot, Grand and Chagrin Rivers, his education is as follows: Ph.D., Purdue University, Department of English. Modern and contemporary American literature with secondary areas in poetry and creative writing. M.A., English, Georgia State University. B.A., University of Maine at Orono, English with a concentration in Classics.

In addition to the poems, he has published articles in *The Drake, The American Fly Fisher, American Angler* and *The Journal of Flyfishing and Tying*.

www.ingramcontent.com/pod-product-compliance
Lightning Source LLC
LaVergne TN
LVHW041507070426
835507LV00012B/1399